First World War
and Army of Occupation
War Diary
France, Belgium and Germany

40 DIVISION
Divisional Troops
244 Machine Gun Company
15 July 1917 - 28 February 1918

WO95/2601/6

The Naval & Military Press Ltd
www.nmarchive.com
Published in association with The National Archives

Published by

The Naval & Military Press Ltd

Unit 10 Ridgewood Industrial Park,

Uckfield, East Sussex,

TN22 5QE England

Tel: +44 (0) 1825 749494

www.naval-military-press.com

www.nmarchive.com

This diary has been reprinted in facsimile from the original. Any imperfections are inevitably reproduced and the quality may fall short of modern type and cartographic standards.

© Crown Copyright
Images reproduced by permission of The National Archives, London, England, 2015.

Contents

Document type	Place/Title	Date From	Date To
Miscellaneous	WO95/260/6		
Heading	40th Division 244th Machine Gun Coy. Jly 1917 1918 Feb		
War Diary	Grantham	15/07/1917	15/07/1917
War Diary	Havre	16/07/1917	18/07/1917
War Diary	Peronne	19/07/1917	19/07/1917
War Diary	Heudecourt	20/07/1917	13/08/1917
War Diary	W6d 6.0 5.1c S.E.	14/08/1917	15/08/1917
War Diary	Trenches	16/08/1917	22/08/1917
War Diary	In Trenches	23/08/1917	29/08/1917
War Diary	Heudecourt	30/08/1917	09/09/1917
War Diary	Beaucamp Villers Ploich Sector	09/09/1917	27/09/1917
War Diary	Heudicourt	28/09/1917	30/09/1917
War Diary	Connelieu-Villers Guislain Sector	30/09/1917	12/10/1917
War Diary	La Herliere	13/10/1917	29/10/1917
War Diary	Warlincourt Lez-Pas	30/10/1917	16/11/1917
War Diary	Laherliere	17/11/1917	17/11/1917
War Diary	Courcelles-Le-Comte	18/11/1917	19/11/1917
War Diary	Beaulencourt	20/11/1917	21/11/1917
War Diary	Le Bucquiere	22/11/1917	23/11/1917
War Diary	Graincourt	23/11/1917	27/11/1917
War Diary	K. 18.b.6.5.	28/11/1917	28/11/1917
War Diary	Blaireville	29/11/1917	03/12/1917
War Diary	Ervillers	04/12/1917	28/02/1918

woasp6016

40TH DIVISION

224TH MACHINE GUN COY.
JLY 1917-~~MAY 1918~~
1918 FEB

ORIGINAL

WAR DIARY
or
INTELLIGENCE SUMMARY.
(Erase heading not required.)

Army Form C. 2118.

No 24th Machine Gun Company
40th Division

Place	Date	Hour	Summary of Events and Information	Remarks and references to Appendices
GRANTHAM	JULY 15th		Left Station at 1.0 AM & with one half at HOLLOWAY for watering animals arrived at SOUTHAMPTON DOCKS 9.45 AM. Embarked all animals & Tpt, cannibals & men, proceeded on board the SS AUSTRALIND at 3 PM. No2. 245, 246 & 247 M.G.Cos passed	
HAVRE	16th		to HAVRE on same boat, arriving 8.30 AM. Company marched to No 1 Rest Camp	
	17th		Completed Store & Ordnance cotton pallets in Utopia, charge for clean it. Pd Installn to No 2 Hospital Cell/ME men & animals paved Jet	
	18th		Entrained at C+RE DES MARCHANDISES & volunteer by rail in Utopia. Entrained at C+RE DES MARCHANDISES & volunteer. 8 Offrs for ore 12 Midd. Some trouble enforcing on entraining animals. Kit bags meatfall	
	19th		from (4.45 - 5.45) at BUCHY where was had Kit bag meatfall	
PERONNE		3 PM	Arrived PERONNE 3 PM. Behaved exceedingly well. Heat provided for. Marched to Reinforcement Camp at QUINCONCE, arriving 5 PM.	
			The men Entrained on light railway & on detrained at 7.0 AM The trainload came by road. Arrived FINS 11.30 AM met by Major LACEY DMGO 40th Division & marched to HEUDECOURT. 1st billet arrived 1.0 PM Lorry	
HEUDECOURT	20th		by road. arrived FINS 11.30 AM met by Major LACEY DMGO 40th Division & marched to HEUDECOURT. 1st billet arrived 1.0 PM Lorry Tpt arrived 4.30 PM Left Guard Room by Divisional Officer.	

Army Form C. 2118.

WAR DIARY
or
INTELLIGENCE SUMMARY.

(Erase heading not required.)

NO 244 Machine Gun Co
4O.C Garrison

Place	Date	Hour	Summary of Events and Information	Remarks and references to Appendices
HEUDECOURT	20th		This Company is attached to the 40th Division as Divisional Machine Gun Coy. Made huts-ten nine beds for all men. Billets on the whole good. Nearly	
	21st		all huts destroyed by the German before leaving.	
			C of E Service on Tpt field. Service interrupted by German aeroplane. Great	
	22nd		held in the Y.M.C.A hut.	
			Company training. Attempts made to hire the Field Canteen, 2nd unsuccessful	
	23rd		Baths at HEUDECOURT & continued with training. Enemy aeroplane active.	
	24th		Played No 120 M.G.Coy at cricket. Won—104 for 5 & got them out for 56.	
	25th		Carried out night firing, range (30yds) with A.A.M. A.A.M.'s unsatisfactory,	
			firing made the machines very fine - holding poor.	
	26th		Training.	
	27th		Training.	
	28th		Training carried out during the morning, and in the afternoon	
			2nd in Command & Section Officers made a reconnaissance	
			of the "Brown" Line.	
	29th		C of E Service, held in a Barn owing to violent thunderstorm.	
			The Divisional Band turned up to render the music, but the	
			inclement weather prevented them from performing	

Army Form C. 2118.

WAR DIARY
or
INTELLIGENCE SUMMARY.

No 244 Machine Gun Coy.
40th Division

(Erase heading not required.)

Place	Date	Hour	Summary of Events and Information	Remarks and references to Appendices
HEUDICOURT	30/7/17	10 AM	The Company was inspected by the G.O.C. 40th Division near 120 M.G. Coy Transport Lines. He expressed himself as pleased with the general appearance of the men then addressing them on parade, and the way they handled their arms. He was also glad to find that the majority of the Officers & N.C.O's had been out before.	
		11.30	Inspection of Billets by G.O.C Division.	
"	31/7/17		Training. 6 Officers & 8. N.C.O's went up the Line for 3 days instruction.	

J. McBee
Lieut.
for O.C. 244 M.G. Coy.

Army Form C. 2118.

No 51 **No. 244 Machine Gun Company.**
10th Division

WAR DIARY
or
INTELLIGENCE SUMMARY.
(Erase heading not required.)

Instructions regarding War Diaries and Intelligence Summaries are contained in F. S. Regs., Part II. and the Staff Manual respectively. Title pages will be prepared in manuscript.

Place	Date	Hour	Summary of Events and Information	Remarks and references to Appendices
HEC D/Coast	Aug 1/8/17		Training – At 7PM No 1 Section left Headquarters and proceeded to take up a section of 120 M.G.Coy at R.19.d.80.60 (57C.SE)/20,000.	
"	2nd		No 2 Section proceeded from Headquarters at 7.30 PM and relieved a section of No 191 Machine Gun Company in No 1 Section relieved section with a section of 119 M.G.Coy taking up a line from R.32.a.93.95 to R.32.d.80.10	
	3rd		Training	
	4th		Training	
	5th	11.30am	Church of England service at 137th Field Ambulance unbegratio.	
	6th		Training	
	7th		Training	
	8th		Section 2 were relieved at 7 PM by a section of 120th M.G.Coy at R.19.d.80.60 (57C). Section 1. were relieved by 2 Cm G/s of 191 M.G.Coy & 2 Lewis guns of 21st Middlesex	
	9th		Training & preparation of winter quarters	
	10		do	
	11		do	
	12	11.30	Church of England Service at 137 F.A. General Borden attended.	

Army Form C. 2118.

WAR DIARY
or
INTELLIGENCE SUMMARY.

(Erase heading not required.)

No 244 Machine Gun Company
40th Division

AUGUST

Instructions regarding War Diaries and Intelligence Summaries are contained in F. S. Regs., Part II. and the Staff Manual respectively. Title pages will be prepared in manuscript.

Place	Date	Hour	Summary of Events and Information	Remarks and references to Appendices
HEUDICOURT	13th	8 p.m.	The Company left their billets at Heudicourt to relieve 119th M.G. Company. By Headquarters in Gorve Ravine (W6d 60)(57c.) No.1 Section placed in Position in Gorve Ravine, No.2 Section in Gouzeaucourt with Left H.Q. at R11 d.10.60 and No.3 & 4 Sections on the Front Line with Right H.Q. at R30 a.8.80. R26 d.60.00 respectively. The relief was reported complete at 1 A.M. 14th inst.	
W6d 6.0 51 c S.E.	14th & 15th		A successful raid was carried out by the Infantry on Beaucamp trenches. Prisoners were captured. Owing to the idiots of our Machine Guns did not take an effective part in the raid. Between 10 & 11 p.m. our out post guns R10 c.12.35 front of the Gouzeaucourt – Villers Guislain road to the sycamore tree. Owing to heavy rain & numbers of infantry in Gorve Ravine making a dugout	
"	15			

WAR DIARY
or
INTELLIGENCE SUMMARY.
(Erase heading not required.)

Army Form C. 2118.

No 244 Machine Gun Coy

Place	Date	Hour	Summary of Events and Information	Remarks and references to Appendices
TRENCHES	16ᵗʰ		Indirect fire on Road from R16.c.00.65 to R16.c.5599 and also 2 guns & also on M.G. emplacement at R15.d.70.12. Situation - normal.	
	17ᵗʰ		Targets engaged R22.b.90.90. R22.b.28.30. R16.a.05.87. & R22.15.60. No ground fires. 9,500. The O.P. in CONNELIEU now in use. A day firing to carried on from R26.b.83. A considerable amount of movement noted behind the line. Indirect action, Relief carried out, No 1 Sec to Right Sub-sects. No 2 to Left Sub-sects. No 3 to FIFTEEN RAVINE. Sect 4 to Coy HQ in company Reserve.	
	18		Target R22.b.35.40. R15.c.80.70. Rounds fired 5000	
	19		Targets engaged. M.G. hostile. R15.d.70.12. & R15.c.65.60. Working party R10.a.28.80 & gap in wire at R15.c.80.60. Rounds fired 9000	
	20		Indirect fire was carried out on R.16.c.60.10. R15.b.70.60. R16.c.70.50. R26.b.90.15. R15.d.70.10 & an M.G. emplacement & gaps in wire which went to the left flank. Rounds expended 12,500.	
	21		Nightfiring was carried out on points detailed every fresh hour. Indirect action relief was carried out without casualties. Rounds fired 16,500.	
	22		A raid by 121ˢᵗ Bat. was arranged to take place in the evening at 4.45 & Barrage on BLEAK SUPPORT with two guns from R19.d.90.50, but cancelled on account of Officers who went over to German trenches will all map to threaten order for the trench raid. A aeroplane was engaged during the day by an aeroplane gun, without visible success.	

WAR DIARY
or
INTELLIGENCE SUMMARY

Army Form C. 2118.

Place	Date	Hour	Summary of Events and Information	Remarks and references to Appendices
IN TRENCHES	Aug 23		Various targets were engaged during the night with indirect fire. Rounds fired 2500.	
"	24		Very quiet. Used gun in a casement. Rounds fired 5000. The shell-hole emplacement aka POPERINGHE is concealed up by camouflaged travel.	
"	25		Gun in war at R15 C 8.1 is being kept open. New enemy M.G. emplacement placed near cross roads landed at R15 C & 90.50. A new cross road CAMBRAI Rd Salient M.G. 7 & 2 is being continuously shelled. A signal rocket was seen at this place at hour day by the R.E. Very quiet night. Rounds fired 9000.	No 84056 Pte DAVIES A buried by shell No 93975 Pte LAMBERT F severely wounded concussion by shell
"	26th		Indirect Section ably both places. Various targets were fired upon during the night. Heavy machine gun M.G. fire. Ammunition expended 5000.	
	27th		Another quiet night. Very large numbers of Germans seen behind Uhlan, particularly in C.32, also activity on their system, several trains near Cambrai COMBRAI FOR CAUDRY. In view of the above machine guns were kept in the emplacement on S.O.S. line. A good deal of shelling on new [sector] in the CAMBRAI Road The hit guns at M.G. 7 & 8 were moved from the position to places on POPE AVENUE, protecting the same area as before. FRIMLEY TRENCH & on off.	

Army Form C. 2118.

WAR DIARY
or
INTELLIGENCE SUMMARY.
(Erase heading not required.)

244 Machine Gun Coy

Place	Date Aug	Hour	Summary of Events and Information	Remarks and references to Appendices
IN TRENCHES	26th		Abnormalist targets moved by machine gun fire throughout the night. Range extended = 14000. M.G.1 & M.G.2 were allotted onwards from CAMBRAI Rd on men of Mt shelling of our barricade over CAMBRAI Rd. 2 Rand men carried out during the night & early morning of 29th & 3rd 17th Welsh & 19th R.W.F. Our machine gun covered as per attached order. The 17th Welsh formed the top portion uncovered & reached unbroken in the bottom portion of nurturing camellia. The 19th R.W.F. secured on prisoner & killed several of the enemy.) M.G. Teamlers having only a few rounds. Rand fired := 10,000. The 119th M.G.Cy relieved us in the trenches. The Cy returning to billet at HEUDECOURT. Relief completed by 12.15 A.M. 30/8/17.	Attached hat No. 98975 Pte LAMBIERT. 17 was found dead at No. 21 PCS on 26th Aug. Buried at V2 a 8 4 Mt. 57.c.
HEUDECOURT	30th		Day spent in cleaning up & inspection of clothing.	
"	31st		Baths at FINS. Kit inspection & checking of all articles in charge to station.	

J. Mebree Lieut
for O.C. 244 Machine Gun Company

Army Form C. 2118.

Vol 3

No 244 Machine Gun Company

WAR DIARY
or
INTELLIGENCE SUMMARY.
(Erase heading not required.)

Place	Date	Hour	Summary of Events and Information	Remarks and references to Appendices
HEUDICOURT	Sept. 1		Training	
"	2		Church Services at HEUDICOURT.	
"	3		Training.	
"	4		Sports Day. The Company held a most successful Sports Day. The first prize winners were as follows:—	
			Rifle shooting — Sgt. Gay.	
			Revolver " — Sgt. Brooks.	
			Throwing Cricket ball. — Pte Nicholson.	
			100 yards flat. — " "	
			220 " " — Johnson H.	
			440 " " — Propes.	
			Obstacle race. — Paling.	
			Mule race. — Boyes	
			Limber driving Competition — Hughill.	
			Football Competition. — Sobriety & Ensign.	
				No. 3 Section.
			Prizes were given by the Officers.	

Army Form C. 2118.

WAR DIARY
or
INTELLIGENCE SUMMARY.
(Erase heading not required.)

244 Machine Gun Company.

Place	Date	Hour	Summary of Events and Information	Remarks and references to Appendices
HEUDICOURT	5		Training.	
"	6		Preparation for trenches. Baths for men.	
		7.30 AM	The Sections left Heudicourt to relieve 120th Machine Gun Coy in the Beaucamp — Villers Plouich Sector. The relief was reported complete at 12.30 AM 7th/9/17. The enemy were very quiet & we did no firing.	
	7th		A mist arose at dawn necessitating extra vigilance on the part of the Sentries.	
night of 7/8th			Crossroads at R3 & 10 90 (57C) were engaged. Arrangements were made to fire on Cuillet Wood but this had to be abandoned on account of our patrols. Infantry reported about 20 of the enemy coming towards our wire but no attack actually took place. 13 Shells dropped in the left of M.G.H. Practically no activity on the front of enemy M. Guns.	
night of 8/9th			Trench in Cuillet engaged from R2 d 05.90 to R2 d 0.5. and also crossroads in R2 d 40.80. Three red lights went up from German lines and a few shells followed. Otherwise a very quiet night.	

(A7092) Wt. W12536/M1293. 75,000. 1/17. D. D. & L. Ltd. Forms/C.2118/14.

WAR DIARY

Army Form C. 2118.

No. 244 Machine Gun Company

Place	Date	Hour	Summary of Events and Information	Remarks and references to Appendices
Leuvrechamps Villers Ploich Sector.	night 9/10th Sept		Night firing from M.G.1 on to R2 600 up to R2 b.0.5 and thence over 3° to left + 7° to right. Between 6pm & 1pm the enemy put some heavy shells into VILLERS PLOICH Expenditure of S.A.A. 2500 rounds.	
	night 10/11th		Inter Section relief carried out. Our guns co-operated with the H.L.I. in a raid on PLOUGH TRENCH. The raiding party returned without securing a prisoner at 1.30 A.M. Expenditure of S.A.A. 5000 rounds.	
	night of 11/12th		The H.L.I. again attempted a raid on PLOUGH TRENCH but failed to secure identification. Our guns co-operated.	
	12th 1 P.M.		Enemy snipers were busy at M.G.3 and wounded the Sentry No. 98943 Pte BARRY J.J. in the right arm.	No 98943 Pte Barry J.J. wounded in right arm.
	night of 12/13 th		The following targets were engaged. Dump - R26.00.50, Cross Roads L.32.C.81.08 - NEW TRENCH. R.2.C.48.15 to R.1.d.05.02. Expenditure of S.A.A. 5000 rounds. Enemy M.Gs were active all night.	

Army Form C. 2118.

WAR DIARY
or
INTELLIGENCE SUMMARY.
(Erase heading not required.)

244 Machine Gun Coy.

Place	Date	Hour	Summary of Events and Information	Remarks and references to Appendices
	Sept			
NIGHT of 13/14th			Concentrations on R3.c.60.70 and R3.c.55.60 at 10.3 P.M. & 10.7 P.M. 2.20 at 10.45 P.M. and 11.30 P.M. 6000 rounds S.A.A. were expended. At 11.20 P.M. the enemy sent over gas shells on to June / station. Bo's respirators were put on & there were no casualties. The S.A.A. was soon dispersed the cloud which was very thin.	
NIGHT of 14/15th			Very quiet night, enemy machine guns very quiet. The Division on our left sent gas over and the enemy retaliated by an artillery bombardment.	
NIGHT of 15/16th			Four of our guns fired concentration on enemy trench at R.9.6.9.8. between 7.30 & 11.5 P.M. Expenditure of S.A.A. 7500 rounds. Enemy machine guns inactive.	
NIGHT of 16/17.			Concentrations were fired on the new enemy work R8.a.65.90 between 9.30 & 11.30 P.M. The road at R3.c.27.30 was also engaged. The enemy retaliated with erratic bursts of Machine Gun fire which however were high. Expenditure of S.A.A. 11,000 rounds.	
		17.50	2000 rounds S.A.A. were fired at enemy aeroplane between 3 & 5 P.M. R.A. was however too far away for our guns to bring them down.	

(A7092) Wt. W.12839/M1293. 75000. 1/17. D. D. & L., Ltd. Forms/C.2118-14.

Army Form C. 2118.

WAR DIARY
or
INTELLIGENCE SUMMARY.
(Erase heading not required)

Instructions regarding War Diaries and Intelligence Summaries are contained in F. S. Regs., Part II. and the Staff Manual respectively. Title pages will be prepared in manuscript.

Place: **No 244 Machine Gun Company**

5.

Place	Date	Hour	Summary of Events and Information	Remarks and references to Appendices
Sept.				
Inight of 17/18th			The following targets were engaged during the night:— Road from R32 c 75.40 to R32 c 75.92. — Road Junction at R3 c 65.90. — Enfiladed communication trench from R1 b 85.50 to R1 b 00.60. Intermittent firing from R3 c to R35 a 9.1. Expenditure of S.A.A. 13,000 rounds.	
Night of 18/19th			Firing carried on according to programme. Expenditure S.A.A. 6700 rounds. Later Section reliefs carried out.	No 98931 L/Cpl. Lewis P. wounded at 8 p.m. 19/9/
Night of 19/20th			Gun was brought to bear on R18 d 40.85. R12 d 15.65. R2 c 85.55. R2 a 15.15. Path on W side of COUILLET WOOD. Road East of RAILWAY R1 b 1.7. R2 c 03.23. L32 c 92.08. Expenditure of S.A.A. 12,000 rounds. Enemy machine guns active	
Night of 20/21st			The following targets were engaged. R1 b 90.20 to R1 b 00.95 (Communication trench), R2 b 48.10 to R2 d 10.50. (Road) also several road running N.E. from R2 d 40.00. L32 a 32.05 (Road to from B2), R1 d 13 Enemy M.G. Pn. R1 d 02.40. This gun was sweeping on target two attempts were located by enemy patrol, the O.C. decide not to fire on it in order to draw on salvos of artillery. When artillery opened fire on fridge to draw it in about 80 secs Bullets were opened to slacken in about 80 secs. S.A.A. for the night 7,500 rounds. 3th. Wilson Lt.

WAR DIARY
or
INTELLIGENCE SUMMARY.
(Erase heading not required.)

Army Form C. 2118.

No 244 M.C. Coy.

Place	Date	Hour	Summary of Events and Information	Remarks and references to Appendices
Night of	Sept 1917 21/22nd		Very quiet night. Targets fired on in @ R1. Expenditure S.A.A. 2000 rds.	
	22nd	7.10. to 8 pm.	This Company cooperated with 14th H.L.I. in a raid on the enemy front line fired from R8.d.6.7. & R8.d.15.90 + the road from R8.d.6.7. to R8.d.75.05. Operation orders attached. 22 Vickers M. Guns fired a total of 101,400 rounds and the average expenditure per gun per minute was 135 rounds.	Report re
Night of	22nd/23rd		The Company was relieved by 120th Machine Gun Company and we went into Divisional reserve at HEUDICOURT.	
	23rd		Day spent in Rest. Clothing Inspection + Baths.	
	24th		Cleaning + blacking all guns, equipment etc.	
	25th		Training + preparation for Trekking.	
Night of	25/26th		Six guns of the Company Co-operated with 121st Machine Gun Coy and Divisional Guy and Divisional fired Guy and fired 6 lines on enemy in support of a raid by the 12th Suffolks. Expenditure of S.A.A. 57,000 round.	
	26th		Training at HEUDICOURT.	
	27th		" "	No 10061 A/Cpl. Porter. F.W. wounded accidental self inflicted.

Army Form C. 2118.

WAR DIARY
or
INTELLIGENCE SUMMARY.

(Erase heading not required.)

244 Machine Gun Coy.

Place	Date	Hour	Summary of Events and Information	Remarks and references to Appendices
HEUDICOURT	Sept 26		Training	
"	29		do.	
"	30		Relieved 121st Machine Gun Company in the CONNELIEU - VILLERS GUISLAIN Sector.	

Mason Lieut
for O.C. 244 M.G. Coy.

Army Form C. 2118.

WAR DIARY
or
INTELLIGENCE SUMMARY.
(Erase heading not required.)

No 244 Machine Gun Coy.

Place	Date	Hour	Summary of Events and Information	Remarks and references to Appendices
CONNELIEU - VILLERS GUISLAIN Sector	night of 30th Sept/1st Oct		Miscellaneous targets were engaged during the night & 12,000 rds ammunition was expended. Enemy M.Gs replied with scattered bursts.	
	night of 1st/2nd Oct		Our guns were very active all night & expended 25,000 rds. Enemy M.Gs only moving west enemy were in R.28.d. (nr. A.57.c) were swept at intervals. During the morning our daylight sniping guns fired on movement in the Rancourt Farm Road.	
	2nd Oct		In cooperation with the Artillery our guns fired concentrations on S.S.C.49. Miscellaneous targets were all engaged & 20,000 rounds were expended.	
	night 2/3/15 - 2/3/10/17		Our guns fired very little owing to friendly patrols.	
	night 3/4th Oct		Our Sniping Gun fired with good effect on movement in RANCOURT FARM ROAD. and at night various targets were engaged. Expenditure of S.A.A. 11,000 rounds. Enemy M.Gs very quiet.	
	4th Oct.		Daylight sniping was again carried out & numerous small parties of the enemy were dispersed.	
	5th Oct.		Our M.Gs put up a feint barrage on BLEAK WALK, BLEAK SUPPORT & BARRACK SUPPORT. in support of a raid by the 119th Infy. Bde. Enemy M.Gs were very active during the retaliation.	
	night of 5/6th Oct.		M.G. movement was sniped at during the day & in all cases hostile dribble ring of enemy 6/4 Oct. Miscellaneous targets were engaged.	

Army Form C. 2118.

WAR DIARY
or
INTELLIGENCE SUMMARY.
(Erase heading not required.)

2. 244th Machine Gun Coy.

Place: CONNELIEU-VILLERS GUISLAIN SECTOR
Date: October 1917.

Place	Date	Hour	Summary of Events and Information	Remarks
CONNELIEU-VILLERS GUISLAIN SECTOR	9th		No 4 Section of this Company entrained in all respects at YTRES for service overseas. 2/Lt. C.G. GLASS to Section Officer. O.B. BENBOW as Sub Section Officer.	
	night 9/10 Oct.		Enemy M.G. posts in R.28 b & R.29A were engaged. Enemy M.G. were active during the early part of the night.	
	night 10/11 Oct		Harassment was fired on during the day on position of enemy in R.29 b. Miscellaneous targets were engaged & 5000 rounds S.A.A. expended.	
	night of 11/12 Oct.		Relieved in the CONNELIEU - VILLERS GUISLAIN Sector by the 61st Machine Gun Coy of the 20th Division. The Company moved back to Billets at HEUDICOURT.	
	12th Oct.		The Transport left HEUDICOURT at 12.30 pm & moved to VII Corps reinforcement billets at O.C. 40th Divisional Train. The remainder of the Company left HEUDICOURT at 2.30 pm by Decauville for PERONNE arrived at PERONNE about 4.30 (MOUNT St DENIS) and marched to billets where we stayed during the night	
	13th Oct		The Company left PERONNE by the 1st Commeter Train at 7.10 am	

Army Form C. 2118.

WAR DIARY
or
INTELLIGENCE SUMMARY. 244th Machine Gun Company.
(Erase heading not required.)

Place	Date	Hour	Summary of Events and Information	Remarks and references to Appendices
	12th	About 2.30 AM	We arrived at the Railhead BEAMETZ-RIVIERE. The Company provided the unloading party. After completion of detraining the Company marched to billets at LA HERLIERE. Map 51C (N10a0.5). Arrived there about 9AM. The transport by road via BAPAUME arrived about 4.30 P.M. (convoy moving by road). Stormy weather. The journey was rather uncomfortable to the men.	
LA HERLIERE	13th		The day was spent in improving billets. Church Service.	
"	14th		Training.	
"	15th		Training.	
"	16th		Training.	
"	17th		Training. The O.C. 40th Divisional Train inspected the 1st Line Transport of the Company and reported as follows:— "H.Q 40th Division Q." I forward herewith report on the Inspection of 1st Line Transport of 244 Machine Gun Coy. on 16/10/17 in accordance with your No 259(Q) dated 12th inst. Animals. Please see attached report of D.A.D.V.S. Harness. In excellent condition, repair, very well kept indeed	

Army Form C. 2118.

WAR DIARY
or
INTELLIGENCE SUMMARY.

(Erase heading not required.)

244 d Machine Gun Coy.

Place	Date	Hour	Summary of Events and Information	Remarks and references to Appendices
LA HERLIERE	18th		Vehicles in good running order & repair. The transport on the whole is in splendid condition & reflects great credit on all concerned. (Sgd) C.E. Leahy, Lt. Col. C.y. 40th Divisional Train A.S.C. 18/10/17. O.C. 40th Divisional Train A.S.C. I forward herewith my remarks on the inspection of transport animals of 244 Machine Gun Coy. for inclusion in your report please. 244 Machine Gun Coy. The Animals are all in good condition and well looked after. There is a great improvement in the shoeing which is now satisfactory. All Animals are under cover. (Sgd) W.V. Rouston, Major A.V.C. D.A.D.V.S 40th Division	
	19th		Training.	

Army Form C. 2118.

WAR DIARY
or
INTELLIGENCE SUMMARY.

244 Machine Gun Company

(Erase heading not required.)

Instructions regarding War Diaries and Intelligence Summaries are contained in F. S. Regs., Part II. and the Staff Manual respectively. Title pages will be prepared in manuscript.

Place	Date	Hour	Summary of Events and Information	Remarks and references to Appendices
LA HERLIÈRE	20th		Leaving. to the Officers the Company played 121st M.G. Coy at Rugby succeeded in letting them 35 pts to 6 pts.	
	21st		Church service.	
	22nd		Training.	
	23rd		Firing on 25 yards range.	
	24th		Firing on 25 yards range.	
	25th		Brigade tactical Scheme.	
	26th		Training	
	27th		"	
	28th		Inspection of Coy Tactical Scheme. Church Parade.	
	29th		At 8 AM the Company vacated their billets in LA HERLIÈRE and marched to WARLINCOURT-LES-PAS.	
WARLINCOURT LES PAS	30 & 31st		Training	

S. McClure, Lieut.
for O.C. 244 Machine Gun Coy.

Army Form C. 2118.

WAR DIARY
or
INTELLIGENCE SUMMARY

No. 244 Machine Gun Company.   Vol 5

Place	Date Nov.	Hour	Summary of Events and Information	Remarks and references to Appendices
WARLINCOURT LEZ-PAS.	1st		Training (Ref map LENS 1/100,000)	
"	2nd		"	
"	3rd		"	
"	4th		Church Parade	
"	5th		Training	
"	6th		"	
"	7th		"	
"	8th		"	
"	9th		"	
"	10th		"	
"	11th		Church Parade	
"	12th		Training	
"	13th		"	
"	14th		"	
"	15th		"	
"	16th	10.30 AM	The Company vacated the billets in WARLINCOURT-LEZ-PAS and marched to LA HERLIÈRE arriving there at 1.5 PM. Billets were occupied in the R.E. Dump.	2/Lt D. MENZIES. left Coy for some leave France
LA HERLIÈRE	17th		The Company left LA HERLIÈRE at 5 PM and marched to COURCELLES-LE-COMTE arriving 11.45 PM. The men were placed in tents & officers had kits.	
COURCELLES LE-COMTE.	18th		Resting, after fifteen days fatiguing march.	
"	19th		Under orders received from 120th Inf. Bde. the Company moved off from COURCELLE LE-COMTE at 7.45 PM in rear of 120th Inf Bde. and marched to BEAULENCOURT	

WAR DIARY
or
INTELLIGENCE SUMMARY

Army Form C. 2118.

244th Machine Gun Company.
40th Division.

NOVEMBER

Place	Date	Hour	Summary of Events and Information	Remarks and references to Appendices
BEAULENCOURT	20th		when they arrived at 12 midnight. Billeted in Nissen huts.	
	20th		The hut at BEAULENCOURT blankets tarpaulin kits were dumped at 120th Infantry Bde dump in the cinema. BEAULENCOURT.	
	21st		The Company became attached to 120th Infantry Brigade and under orders from them huded H.Q. from BEAULENCOURT at 2.15 P.M. and arrived at LEBUCQUIÈRE at 5 PM. The Company occupied tents.	
LEBUCQUIÈRE	22nd		Standing to at LEBUCQUIÈRE all day, at night received orders to march off at 4.40 A.M. 23/11/17	
	23rd		The Company marched off to MÉTZ-EN-COUTURE (?) 120th Infantry Bde to the HINDENBURG SUPPORT in K10d. (Ref.m.p. MŒUVRES 20,000.) at which point they arrived at 11 AM. Crossed the Canal at K15a. At 1PM the Company received orders to fall back in certainly to go into billets of 23rd/24th Nov 1917. The O.C. got into touch with H.Q. 119th + 121st Infantry Bdes in the Church at GRAINCOURT. The Section officers got into touch with 119th and 121st Machine Gun Coys. Section officers returned at 4.30 PM and took their sections into etabl. No 1 Section attached M.G Coy on the left + Section 2 + 3 + No. 4 M.Guns of Coy on the right at 10.30 A.M. No. 119 H + 121st Bdes attacked BOURLON WOOD succeeded in establishing a line just below US M edge of BOURLON WOOD	

Army Form C. 2118.

WAR DIARY
or
INTELLIGENCE SUMMARY

(Erase heading not required.)

Instructions regarding War Diaries and Intelligence Summaries are contained in F. S. Regs., Part II. and the Staff Manual respectively. Title pages will be prepared in manuscript.

NOVEMBER

Place	Date	Hour	Summary of Events and Information	Remarks and references to Appendices
GRAINCOURT	28th		No.1 Section under the orders of 12th & 11th Bde placed together at E23.d 2.1 (M.R.B. MOEUVRES 1/20,000) covering the road on SDS line from the CRUCIFIX B13 - No QUARRY - E3. Initially the Left flank of the Bde was taken & as under the orders of the 119th Infantry Bde took up positions at E30.d.0.8. respectively at N9 & Pits on F21.c respectively. The 1st Bn Scots Guards were later moved to the EASTERN EDGE of BOURLON WOOD also covering the CAMBRAI ROAD. HQ remained at K10.d 3.9. The transport lines about K15.b.6.5. Section 1 moved to E23.d.09 with a barrage mgk. at 3.0 PM when an attack on BOURLON VILLAGE & crest of BOURLON WOOD. At same from Left Sec made a NE Section also took up F.gun E11.a 4.0 to E11.a 3.4 for 2 guns. Lifted to F gun of 131 MC6) will have an own area. The section was under shell fire from a NE direction during its stay here considerably. A Lowbardment at 6 AM but none of the guns suffered any & adverse to action of the nineteen lines. Men were called upon to put down a barrage. Section 2 inundated continuously throughout the day & ammon of the infantry were relying from the road by Lt BONNITZ 11 of 1st Bn Scots arranged 2 guns at F13.d.0.6 covering the southern edge of BOURLON WOOD, at 6 PM L. received orders to report to Col BENZIES Runners mounted through an enemy barrage. These were 6 casualties. The On BENZIES being no unit at and Lt set with Lt Section to reply out at F9.A.1.2. When am moved from	Wounded No 43158 Pte MALEN L/Cpl [?] No. 63515 Pte BOYLET No 99403 Pte BARRY J J No 108944 Pte PINCH H No 57977 Pte HOLDSWORTH No 99642 Pte THOMSON A No 97986 Pte WOOLHEAD W

WAR DIARY or INTELLIGENCE SUMMARY

Army Form C. 2118.

NOVEMBER   No. 2nd M.G.Cy

Place	Date	Hour	Summary of Events and Information	Remarks and references to Appendices
GRAINCOURT	24th		O.C. 119 M.G.Cy to mount his guns along the CAMBRAI Rd to cover exit from ravine & the road towards FONTAINE-NOTRE-DAME, as the infantry were retiring on the right of the road. An infantry to the BOURLON WOOD were away & to be informed of the intention had now retired & the infantry were holding the eastern outskirts to dig in. At Section 3 at the X Rd in FABC fired 5000 rounds on the SOS being first. Rabin were delivered 15 Section in fact made; one made was lost at the CRUCIFIX after being wounded.	Nº 369 Dr BARTON Nº 17953 Pr HALL J Nº 97354 Pr WATSON S Signals Nº 177515-S Nº 50498 Dr STEWART W Nº 41652 Dr JOHNSTONE A No 21485 Pr BROWN A Nº 91124 Pr FEARN R PTE S.G. WHITAKER (no ref) (no ref) Sergt PRATT F (on duty) Nº 104063 Pr HAMILTON G
"	25th		[illegible handwritten entry continues]	

5

Instructions regarding War Diaries and Intelligence Summaries are contained in F. S. Regs., Part II. and the Staff Manual respectively. Title pages will be prepared in manuscript.

NOVEMBER

WAR DIARY
or
~~INTELLIGENCE SUMMARY.~~
(Erase heading not required.)

Army Form C. 2118.

No 244 Machine Gun Coy

Place	Date	Hour	Summary of Events and Information	Remarks and references to Appendices
GRAINCOURT	25th		Sait F7d 23, also a small party coming from their immediate front. Fire was opened, the position dispersed. One man was seen about 20x away & one of the gunners went out & brought him in as a prisoner. An enemy machine gun about F7d 4045 caused many casualties. The 119th Bde was relieved by the 167th Bde. Two of our guns were put out of action & having only 2 guns left & 5 men, 2/Lt BOWKER asked to be relieved. The reply to the effect that he was to return to Coy HQ never reached him, so he hung on until the night of the 26th when by permission of the CO 2/6th YORKS he evacuated his position & made his way to HAVRINCOURT where he was found on the morning of the 28th having [illegible] & traced HQ 244 MG Coy.	
			Section 3 opened fire on their SOS lines at 1.00 PM & his position were shelled causing casualties. On their right the Guards Div were conducting a [illegible] Bde relief & both their Transport rolled past their position with the result that they were again shelled with further casualties.	
	26th		The Company was now under the orders of the DMGO (MAJOR [illegible] MC) 62nd Division. Nothing of importance to report. The men were by this time much fatigued particularly those of Section 3 who had no protection of any sort from shell fire, wind & bad weather.	
	27th		Section 1 placed a barrage with guns of this Company on a line from the CRUCIFIX to the QUARRY covering the left flank of an attack by the 186th & 187th Bde & guarded them from 6.20 to 6.40 AM & from 11.0 AM to 1.0 PM. They were heavily shelled. Section 3 did not fire but were troubled very much by shell fire & machine gun fire one man being wounded by a bullet & others by shells. Orders were	No 99624 Pte BURNARD No 99550 Pte CAMPBELL J. No 99622 Pte JOHNSTON W.

Army Form C. 2118.

WAR DIARY
or
INTELLIGENCE SUMMARY.
(Erase heading not required.)

No 244 Machine Gun Coy

Instructions regarding War Diaries and Intelligence Summaries are contained in F. S. Regs., Part II. and the Staff Manual respectively. Title pages will be prepared in manuscript.

NOVEMBER

Place	Date	Hour	Summary of Events and Information	Remarks and references to Appendices
GRAINCOURT	27th		Section of the Coy to commence the position as soon after dark as possible & the Section inoculated at Tpt Lines. Sectn 3 were shelled all the way out to COSTICE. Our Section Officer states very highly of their man, many of whom had never previously been instructed. Several casualties, several men having been made of: Sectn 1 - Pte WEBSTER - 2 - Pte THOMAS E - 3 - Pte PIERSON Pte BURNE Pte PORTER Pte BARKER Pte HUNTER The Section Officer worked out the details in an exemplary way & all the men after ample 2/Lt POWERS displayed ability notable in the laying of the gun in BOURLON WOOD Copy of letter received from 40° Div. The General Commanding sends the attached copy of his letter had it received from the Army Commander shown to officers. Lt Col Burton & Machine Gun Company for the consideration that great credit is due to the fine fighting qualities & endurance displayed by them during the recent operations. Signed W.C. CHARLES Lt Col "b" General Staff 40° Div 28/11/17 COPY. HQ 3rd Army B.E.F My dear Ponsonby Wireless may be the final result of the situation as a whole. I cannot let the particular period of it have without sending you a line to convey my most sincere congratulations on your feat of arms. The captain of	NOVEMBER Pte LONDON J M/259583 To CARROT

WAR DIARY
or
INTELLIGENCE SUMMARY

Army Form C. 2118.

NOVEMBER

No 204 Machine Gun Co

Place	Date	Hour	Summary of Events and Information	Remarks and references to Appendices
GRAINCOURT	27th		BOURLON WOOD stands out amongst all the splendid actions of our Infantry since the gallant start on the 20th & by years to come Infantry soldiers will remember with unqualified admiration the fine response of the splendid gunner with which I have invariably associated for some time. My sincerest thanks for the continued success and my best congratulations. Yours Sincerely signed J BYNG 29/11/17	
RIBS & S	28th		All waiting for horses arrived at 8.32 & Column moved down by own transport from HERMIES. The Coy moved off at 11 AM & marched to MŒUFRES Ng M1772 where been picked the men up & led them to BAPAUME arriving 4.30 PM. Chardeaune arrived at 4.30 PM & marched on to Jeds between BLAIREVILLE & HENDECOURT arriving 8 PM. The Transport came by road. Returned to 40th DIVISION. In Rest & nothing to Transport arrived at 4 PM.	
BLAIREVILLE	29th			
	30th		Cleaning up. & refilling both. Received orders to be prepared to mount & have all at 80 PM. No movement made and remain during the night.	

signed Maurice C. Perfect
o.c.
No 204 M.C. Coy

Maurice C. Perfect Capt
No 204 M.C. Coy

Army Form C. 2118.

WAR DIARY
or
INTELLIGENCE SUMMARY.
(Erase heading not required.)

No 244 Machine Gun Coy Vol 6

DECEMBER

Place	Date	Hour	Summary of Events and Information	Remarks and references to Appendices
BLAIREVILLE	1st		Nothing of importance to report. Details in training.	
	2nd		Training. Gunner A. 99976 Pte Steen S. died of wounds 26.11.17. 99980 Pte Shall J. died of wounds	
	3rd		Bfr BLAIREVILLE at 8 am & proceeded to BELFAST CAMP, ERVILLERS. Captain Cooper went with them	
ERVILLERS	4th		Box other ranks returned from the M.G.C Base Depot CAMIERS. Training, up equipment & cleaning	
	5th		One other rank reported from M.G.C. Base Depot CAMIERS. Training	
	6th		2/Lieut HOWARD. B. reported from M.G.C Base Depot CAMIERS. Training	
	7th		Washing parties. Sunday	
	8th		20 other ranks reported from M.G.C. Base Depot CAMIERS. Testing guns & supplies. Football in the afternoon	
	9th		Church parade.	
	10th		Received 142"/118. Coy. G.H.Q B+ S&T right sector. Relief uncompleted by 5.15 P.M. the Bn we relieve. The Battalion Commander was in command had difficulty	
			Hostile M. Guns fired intermittently during the night all the guns stood to from 3.30 a.m. Sang to support enemy trench & no mans land to sweep	
			Enemy increased rate of Vickers trench & no mans land to sweep	
	11th		Heavy bombardment by German artillery fell on our lines 6/12 5am. 12 = & continued until 8/15am. S.O.S signal went up from right posts and all our guns opened out at once. An infantry attack took	

WAR DIARY
or
INTELLIGENCE SUMMARY
(Erase heading not required.)

Army Form C. 2118.

Place	Date	Hour	Summary of Events and Information	Remarks and references to Appendices
	13/5	1.5 am	Enemy sent over a large number of gas shells, mixed with heavy explosive, had to be worn for an hour. S.O.S. signal went up on our right at 6.30 am & the artillery carried out bombardment the high ground beyond Bellecourt. Intermittent shelling both ways all day long.	
	14/5		Very quiet day. Enemy shelled between Loupart about 1st Sqn & 2nd Sqn. Also a few shells fell on Ferfay at Rue about Lnl Spm & 9.30 pm.	
	15/5		Battn. relieved 119 = Infantry Brigade in an attack. Carried out by 11 pm on following morning. Two 18 pounder guns by our Left Coy's Lewis gun opened fire at 30pm & two guns manned by 119 = Inf Bgd guns were fired 12.30 on wards. No casualties reported to Bgd HQ. Enemy barrage fell at 3.25 pm & continued until about 4.0 pm.	
	16/5		Fairly quiet day. Enemy sent a few shells near the Battn HQ dug in sq 37 x 38, and trenches 9.0 pm a few fell on our front line. Night firing by our guns on to our front of front line. Route used from W9c0818 to W15a2690; also some tanks on route used from W9c0818 to W15a2690. U.9.L.3030.	

Army Form C. 2118.

WAR DIARY
or
INTELLIGENCE SUMMARY.
(Erase heading not required.)

Place	Date	Hour	Summary of Events and Information	Remarks and references to Appendices
	17/12/17		Register [illegible] observed [illegible]. Night firing task (known Gulleries, tracks, Road Juncs U.9.B. 30.30 Strongpoints U.9.a. 79.62. 500 rounds expended.	
	18/12/17		Quiet day. Night shelling on forward area but by known targets. Hostile shelling gun pits very heavy during the previous night. Building of a wet-during table commenced at H.Q.	G Kellys Hangar at Bde H.Q. from Infantry Bnor. Pleasant 4.0 pm
	19/12/17		The Brigade was relieved by 119 Bde. By and returned to billets in Billet Camp Emittes.	
	20/12/17		Inspections and Training.	
	21/12/17		Inspections and Training.	
	22/12/17		Inspection of the Brigade by Lt Genl Cumberlain commanding VI Corps on the importance of steadier guns.	Address to Officers and
	23/12/17		Church Parades.	
	24/12/17		Training.	

Army Form C. 2118.

WAR DIARY
or
INTELLIGENCE SUMMARY.
(Erase heading not required.)

244th Machine Gun Company

December 1917.

Place	Date	Hour	Summary of Events and Information	Remarks and references to Appendices
	25/12/17		Church Parade and Football. Other Christmas Games in Y.M.C.A. Griffiths. at 1.45 p.m. Men thoroughly enjoyed their feast. 7th water Change from river front to snow and hail.	
	26/12/17		Training.	
	27th		do.	
	28th		do.	
	29th		The Company vacated their Quarters in Belfast Camp ERVILLERS and moved to Dugout line South of ERVILLERS. Sections were billeted in DYSART CAMP between ERVILLERS & MORY.	
	30th		A complete M.G. Section joined the Company to replace the Section which provided overseas to another front. Lieut. W.F. Amesden Section officer 2/Lt. Pirrie as Sect-Section Officer. During the morning the Company (no 1 Section) made preparations to repair the Night Machine Gun Company (No. 2 Section) Section moved off from DYSART CAMP at 12.30 P.M and the relief was reported complete at 5 P.M.	
	31st		Desultory shelling of the front and machine guns very quiet.	

R. Meloney
Lt M.G. Coy.
for O.C. 244

Army Form C. 2118.

WAR DIARY
or
INTELLIGENCE SUMMARY
(Erase heading not required.)

No. 244 MACHINE GUN COMPANY.

JANUARY 1918.

Instructions regarding War Diaries and Intelligence Summaries are contained in F. S. Regs., Part II. and the Staff Manual respectively. Title pages will be prepared in manuscript.

Place	Date	Hour	Summary of Events and Information	Remarks and references to Appendices
	1st		The Company is under the command orders of G.O.C. 119th Infantry Bde. Our Machine Gun extended in ammunition. Enemy M.G. fired intermittently during day & night. Hostile artillery was fairly quiet. Enemy aircraft active.	
	2nd		Afternoon. Enemy traffic & a few gas shells near M.G. positions 40.1 & 40.2. The new teams from England were attached to gun teams for 24 hours machine gun.	
	3rd		There was rather more enemy shelling than usual and hostile trench mortars were very busy between 9.30 & 10.30 A.M. Enemy aircraft were active & 2 bombs dropped near M.G. 39A. One or two gas shells fell during the evening.	
	4th		Hostile Machine Guns were very quiet but artillery very active with occasional half an hour bombardments. There was a very heavy bombardment on our left (34th Div. front) between 10 & 10.45 PM. Enemy again put a few gas shells over at intervals.	
	5th		Enemy bombarded Old Sector E. of Bullecourt at 6 AM. S.O.S. was sent up at 6.30 AM. all our guns on that front opened fire. Hostile M. G. were quiet but artillery was very active between 9.30 P.M. & 11.30 P.M.	

Army Form C. 2118.

WAR DIARY
INTELLIGENCE SUMMARY.
(Erase heading not required.)

Instructions regarding War Diaries and Intelligence Summaries are contained in F. S. Regs., Part II. and the Staff Manual respectively. Title pages will be prepared in manuscript.

Place	Date	Hour	Summary of Events and Information	Remarks and references to Appendices
	6th		Mainly quiet day with occasional 10 minute bombardments by the enemy artillery which included a few Gas shells.	
	7th		Company wrenched in the line by 119th M.G. Coy. & marched to billets in DYSART CAMP.	
	8th		Cleaning of guns, equipment, clothing, vehicles, spare parts.	
	9th 10th		Training, Lewis gunners, Limbers Training + testing guns on the Range	
	11th		Training. Inspection of First Aid Haversacks of 11th 12th 13th. The Company "Stood to" (Expecting enemy infantry attack) in view of an anticipated attack in strength by the enemy in this Sector from 6.30AM to 7.30AM.	
	12th		Training. Copies of Report. Animals very good. Harness very good & well cared for. Vehicles in good serviceable condition, a few minor repairs required.	
	13th		Training	
	14th		Training	
	15th		The Captain Coo, 1 Section relieved the 120th M.G. Coy. (Reserve Section) in the Line Right Sector. Company HQ was at C9d80.60. Sections 3 took up positions North of ECOUST.	
			The relief was carried out with great difficulty owing to the sudden thaw followed by a deluge of rain.	

Army Form C.2118a.

Army Form C. 2118.

WAR DIARY
or
INTELLIGENCE SUMMARY.
(Erase heading not required.)

No. 244 Machine Gun Coy.

January 1918

Instructions regarding War Diaries and Intelligence Summaries are contained in F. S. Regs., Part II. and the Staff Manual respectively. Title pages will be prepared in manuscript.

Place	Date	Hour	Summary of Events and Information	Remarks and references to Appendices
III	16th		The trenches were impassable owing to the thaw and all movement had to be made over the top. The enemy were clearly visible and were evidently unable to use their trenches. There was very little artillery activity.	
	17th		The trenches were still in a very bad condition. There was intermittent artillery activity during the day and Railway Reserve was shelled until 5.9" during the early part of the night.	
	18th		There was a slight improvement in the weather but the trenches were still not fit to be used. Visibility was good and a certain amount of aeroplane activity took place which resulted in the serious damage of one German plane.	
	19th		There was a marked improvement in the condition of the trenches and most of the movement over the top during daylight was discontinued. There was intermittent artillery activity on both sides. Several 77 m.m. shells fell near our "B" Position during the night.	
	20th		There was nothing of interest to report on this day. Artillery on both sides was quiet. Third Army slight aeroplane activity.	
	21st		Artillery on both sides was more active. Our No. 1 Section Head Quarters in Gotha Alley was shelled considerably during the afternoon. The condition of the trenches was again slightly improved.	
	22nd		Snipers on both sides were active. Lieut. Hilken was wounded by rifle fire and was evacuated.	
	23rd		The company less one section was relieved by the 180 Company less one section and	

Army Form C. 2118.

WAR DIARY
or
INTELLIGENCE SUMMARY.
(Erase heading not required.)

No 244 MACHINE GUN COMPANY

JANUARY 1918

Instructions regarding War Diaries and Intelligence Summaries are contained in F.S. Regs., Part II. and the Staff Manual respectively. Title pages will be prepared in manuscript.

Place	Date	Hour	Summary of Events and Information	Remarks and references to Appendices
IV	23rd		Proceeded to DURROW CAMP MORY.	
	24th		Cleaning of guns and equipment. Checking of spare parts. No 3 Section position was Actively bombarded from 9.30 A.M. to 12.15 A.M. Nos 1 & 2 Sections were employed in digging emplacements behind the line.	
	25th		" "	
	26th		No 4 Section relieved No 3 Section and No 3 Section returned to DURROW CAMP MORY.	
	27th		No 1 & 2 Sections were employed in digging emplacements behind the line.	
	28th		" "	
	29th		" "	
	30th		" "	
	31st		The Company less one Section relieved 119 Coy. less one Section in the Left Sector. No 4 Section relieved a Section of 119 Coy in PELICAN AVENUE and the former Section returned to the position N of Ecoust. Company Headquarters was situated in ST LEGER.	

W Amoden
Lt. P.a. O.C. 244 M.G. Coy.

Army Form C. 2118.

WAR DIARY
or
INTELLIGENCE SUMMARY.

No. 244 MACHINE GUN COMPANY.

FEBRUARY 1918

Place	Date	Hour	Summary of Events and Information	Remarks and references to Appendices
1.	1st.		Intermittent artillery activity on both sides and intermittent hostile machine gun fire during the night.	
	2nd		Intermittent artillery activity on both sides. Our machine guns fired 3,000 rounds during the night on the approaches to HENDECOURT.	
	3rd		Artillery on both sides was quiet. Our machine guns fired 2,000 rounds during the night on the approaches to HENDECOURT. Enemy aircraft were active during the night.	
	4th		Enemy heavily shelled our gun positions at the top of PELICAN AVENUE. Our machine guns fired 1500 rounds at cross roads W. of HENDECOURT.	
	5th		Enemy shelled our gun positions in PELICAN AVENUE intermittently during the morning and our positions in CRUX ROAD were shelled at 4 A.M and 9 P.M. Intermittent hostile machine gun fire during the night.	
	6th		At 10 A.M. and 4 P.M enemy shelled in the vicinity of our 30 and 34 positions. Hostile machine guns were active during the night.	
	7th		Artillery on both sides very quiet throughout the day. Intermittent hostile machine gun fire during the night. Our machine guns fired 2,000 rounds at cross roads W. of HENDECOURT between 6 P.M and 9 P.M.	
	8th		At 6.30 A.M the S.O.S signal went up and all our guns fired on S.O.S lines opened fire immediately. Fire was ceased at 7.30 A.M. Enemy artillery retaliated especially on our position in PELICAN AVENUE. The remainder of the day was very quiet.	
	9th			
	10th		Our machine guns fired 2,000 rounds during the night at various roads W. of HENDECOURT. Hostile machine guns fired intermittently during the early part of the night and the early part of the morning. Artillery on both sides kept quiet.	

Army Form C. 2118.

WAR DIARY
or
INTELLIGENCE SUMMARY

(Erase heading not required.) No. 244. MACHINE GUN COY.

Instructions regarding War Diaries and Intelligence Summaries are contained in F. S. Regs., Part II. and the Staff Manual respectively. Title pages will be prepared in manuscript.

Place	Date	Hour	Summary of Events and Information	Remarks and references to Appendices
	FEBRUARY. 1916.			
	11th		Intermittent artillery fire on both sides. Intermittent machine gun fire hostile during the night.	
	12th		The company was relieved in the line by 115th Machine Gun Coy, and proceeded to billets in DUKROW. CAMP MORY.	
	13th		Cleaning of guns, gun kit, mens clothing & equipment. Checking of mens kits.	
	14th		Cleaning & greasing of limbers. Resetting of huts fatigue.	
	15th		Inspection of mens equipment by O/c. Coy; Training.	
	16th		Training. Recreational Training	
	17th		Reconnaissance of Reserve Machine Gun Positions by Coy; Officers and N.C.O's and Church Parade. Recreational Training.	
	18th		Training.	
	19th		Improvements and erecting of baled wire entanglements at reserve machine gun emplacements	
	20th		Inspection by O/c company of returns in Full Marching Order. Recreational Training. Resetting of huts.	
	21st			
	22nd		Cos: 8laying of reserve machine gun emplacements. Checking	
	23rd		Inspection of Company whilst training by Div: Machine Gun Batt: Commander. Fortunes of Battle lines	

A7091. Wt. W1289/M1992 750. Jy. 1117. D. D & L., Ltd. Forms/C2118/14.

Army Form C. 2118.

WAR DIARY
or
INTELLIGENCE SUMMARY

(Erase heading not required.) No. 244 MACHINE GUN COMPANY.

FEBRUARY 1916

Place	Date	Hour	Summary of Events and Information	Remarks and references to Appendices
	24th		Church Parades.	
	25th		Training: Formation of 40th Divisional Machine Gun Battalion.	
	26th		Revetments of huts. Recreational Training.	
	27th		The company was relieved at DURROW CAMP. by 121st Machine Gun Coy and proceeded to DURHAM CAMP. The company will in future be known as D. coy, 40th Divisional Machine Gun Battalion. (late 244th Machine Gun Coy).	
	28th		Training: Reconnaissance of Reserve Battery Positions, to be occupied in case of alarm, by Section Officers and N.C.Os. Recreational Training for the men.	

Melville
Lieut & O.C.
"D" COMPANY
late No. 244 MACHINE GUN COY.

www.ingramcontent.com/pod-product-compliance
Lightning Source LLC
Chambersburg PA
CBHW081247170426
43191CB00037B/2075